international regulations for preventing collisions at sea

1972
International Regulations
for Preventing
Collisions at Sea

*Annotated for yachtsmen
by Bill Anderson*

In force 15th July 1977

Updated 1995

An RYA publication

Published by
The Royal Yachting Association
Tel: 0845 345 0400
Email: admin@rya.org.uk
Web: www.rya.org.uk

© 1988 Royal Yachting Association and W.S.B. Anderson
All rights reserved. No part of this publication may be transmitted, stored in a retrieval system, or transmitted, in any form or by any means, electronic, mechanical, photocopying, recording or otherwise, without the prior permission of the publisher.

CONTENTS

PART D SOUND AND LIGHT SIGNALS

PART E EXEMPTIONS

ANNEX

ANNEX I Positioning and Technical Details of Lights and Shapes

ANNEX II Additional Signals for Vessels Fishing in Close Proximity

ANNEX III Technical Details of Sound Signal Appliances

ANNEX IV Distress Signals

INTRODUCTION

This RYA book has been prepared particularly with the skipper of a *pleasure craft* in mind. The notes beneath certain of the rules are intended to emphasise some aspects which are particularly important to yachtsmen and to show how they apply to practical situations which may arise at sea.

The general rules and the steering and sailing rules, are so much a part of general seamanship and navigation that the idea of having to refer to the *rule book* at sea is as ridiculous as suggesting that frequent reference should be made to the seamanship and navigation manuals while sailing. There is no particular virtue in committing the rules to memory but everyone who goes to sea in a responsible capacity should be sufficiently familiar with the rules to be able to abide by the spirit of all of them.

The ability to recognise groups of lights, day signals and sound signals is also essential. It is impractical to consider consulting a light recognition book on a wet and stormy night at sea. A knowledge of the significance of any group of lights is an essential prerequisite to the application of the steering and sailing rules.

The RYA gratefully acknowledges the permission of the Inter-Governmental Maritime Organization (IMO) to reprint the International Regulations for Preventing Collisions at Sea and the assistance of those who compiled the notes to the Rules.

Note that there will be some minor changes coming into effect in November 2003 which have reference to Wing in Ground(WIG) aircraft.

PART A GENERAL

Rule 1
Application

(a) These Rules shall apply to all vessels upon the high seas and in all waters connected therewith navigable by seagoing vessels.

(b) Nothing in these Rules shall interfere with the operation of special rules made by an appropriate authority for roadsteads, harbours, rivers, lakes or inland waterways connected with the high seas and navigable by seagoing vessels. Such special rules shall conform as closely as possible to these Rules.

(c) Nothing in these Rules shall interfere with the operation of any special rules made by the Government of any State with respect to additional station or signal lights, shapes or whistle signals for ships of war and vessels proceeding under convoy, or with respect to additional station or signal lights or shapes for fishing vessels engaged in fishing as a fleet. These additional station or signal lights, shapes or whistle signals shall, so far as possible, be such that they cannot be mistaken for any light, shape or signal authorized elsewhere under these Rules.

(d) Traffic separation schemes may be adopted by the Organization for the purpose of these Rules.

(e) Whenever the Government concerned shall have determined that a vessel of special construction or purpose cannot comply fully with the provisions of any of these Rules with respect to the number, position, range or arc of visibility of lights or shapes, as well as to the disposition and characteristics of sound signalling appliances, such vessel shall comply with such other provisions in regard to the number, position, range of arc of visibility of lights or shapes, as well as to the disposition and characteristics of sound signalling appliances, as her Government shall have determined to be the closest possible compliance with these Rules in respect of that vessel.

Note to Rule 1

Many harbour authorities have local regulations which apply within their harbour limits These concern such things as special local sound signals for vessels manoeuvring, and priorities for vessels bound inward or outward. The Admiralty Sailing Directions which are brought up to date every 18 months or so by the issue of a supplement give details of most local regulations and should be consulted before entering an unfamiliar harbour.

The special signals referred to under Rule 1(c) are not often encountered but details of those which exist will be found in the annual summary of Admiralty Notices to Mariners.

Traffic separation schemes are an increasingly important feature in the regulation and control of shipping movements and are therefore specifically referred to under Rule 1(d). The lanes and zones which make up separation schemes are shown on the Admiralty charts of the areas in which they are in operation.

Many warships, for example, carry either fewer lights than are required or lights which are positioned in an unusual way. A submarine carries its steaming lights much lower than a vessel of her size is required to do by the regulations and at night this gives the impression that she is much farther away than she actually is. Other classes of warship carry their steaming lights very close together which makes it extremely difficult to judge their aspect. The existence of these unusual lights means that assumptions must not be made simply from the appearance of another ship's lights.

Rule 2
Responsibility

(a) Nothing in these Rules shall exonerate any vessel, or the owner, master or crew thereof, from the consequences of any neglect to comply with these Rules or of the neglect of any precaution which may be required by the ordinary practice of seamen, or by the special circumstances of the case.

(b) In construing and complying with these Rules due regard shall be had to all dangers of navigation and collision and to any special circumstances, including the limitations of the vessels involved, which may make a departure from these Rules necessary to avoid immediate danger.

Note to Rule 2

Rules do not prevent collisions. Those in charge of ships make decisions based upon Rules and it is their decisions which prevent collisions. It is important when considering the regulations to consider also the context in which they have to be applied. Their purpose is to establish a code of conduct for ships at sea so that lights and signals are identifiable, manoeuvres to avoid collisions conform to a predictable pattern and vessels are navigated in such a way that all reasonable safety precautions are taken. No regulation gives right-of-way to any ship. Right-of-way is only given by one ship when it alters course or speed for another and, although (hopefully) ships will alter course and speed as required by the regulations, everyone at sea has an equal responsibility to avoid collision. The regulations are only one of a number of factors which govern the conduct of a ship at sea and cannot be applied without reference to a particular navigational situation or the handling characteristics of the ships or boats involved.

Rule 3
General definitions

For the purpose of these Rules, except where the context otherwise requires:

(a) The word *vessel* includes every description of water craft, including non-displacement craft and seaplanes, used or capable of being used as a means of transportation on water.

(b) The term *power-driven vessel* means any vessel propelled by machinery.

(c) The term *sailing vessel* means any vessel under sail provided that propelling machinery, if fitted, is not being used.

(d) The term *vessel engaged in fishing* means any vessel fishing with nets, lines, trawls or other fishing apparatus which restrict manoeuvrability, but does not include a vessel fishing with trolling lines or other fishing apparatus which do not restrict manoeuvrability.

(e) The word *seaplane* includes any aircraft designed to manoeuvre on the water.

(f) The term *vessel not under command* means a vessel which through some exceptional circumstance is unable to manoeuvre as required by these Rules and is therefore unable to keep out of the way of another vessel.

(g) The term *vessel restricted in her ability to manoeuvre* means a vessel which from the nature of her work is restricted in her ability to manoeuvre as required by these Rules and is therefore unable to keep out of the way of another vessel.

The term *vessels restricted in their ability to manoeuvre* shall include but not be limited to:

(i) a vessel engaged in laying, servicing or picking up a navigation mark, submarine cable or pipeline;

(ii) a vessel engaged in dredging, surveying or underwater operations;

(iii) a vessel engaged in replenishment or transferring persons, provisions or cargo while underway;

(iv) a vessel engaged in the launching or recovery of aircraft;

(v) a vessel engaged in mine clearance operations;

(vi) a vessel engaged in a towing operation such as severely restricts the towing vessel and her tow in their ability to deviate from their course.

(h) The term *vessel constrained by her draught* means a power-driven vessel which, because of her draught in relation to the available depth and width of navigable water, is severely restricted in her ability to deviate from the course she is following.

(i) The word *underway* means that a vessel is not at anchor, or made fast to the shore, or aground.

(j) The words *length* and *breadth* of a vessel mean her length overall and greatest breadth.

(k) Vessels shall be deemed to be in sight of one another only when one can be observed visually from the other.

(l) The term *restricted visibility* means any condition in which visibility is restricted by fog, mist, falling snow, heavy rainstorms, sandstorms or any other similar causes.

Note to Rule 3

The list of definitions gives precise meaning to a number of words which have particular significance. Rule 3(c) is noteworthy for yachtsmen.

SECTION I
Conduct of vessels in any condition of visibility
Rule 4
Application
Rules in this Section apply in any condition of visibility.

Rule 5
Look-out
Every vessel shall at all times maintain a proper look-out by sight and hearing as well as by all available means appropriate in the prevailing circumstances and conditions so as to make a full appraisal of the situation and of the risk of collision.

Note to Rule 5
This is the most important Rule. If it is not observed, the rest of the Rules might as well not exist.

In a sailing yacht there are two potential blind arcs, on the lee bow and directly to windward. Low-clewed, long-footed headsails create a very large blind arc. Even a relatively high-clewed sail can have a similar effect when the yacht is well heeled. This blind arc is worst for crew members sitting to windward in the cockpit. A really effective look-out can often be kept, only if one member of the watch on deck sits to leeward, well aft in the cockpit.

The windward blind arc only exists in strong winds when the spray and rain sting the eyes. It is painful to look directly up-wind in a blow. Even the best designed oilskins will not keep the spray out in a full frontal attack, so the natural instinct to stay dry does not encourage a good watch to windward. Oilskin hoods do not help much; if they are loose fitting enough to be comfortable they will not turn with the head. Looking over one's shoulder for a quick glance up-wind results only in a close-up view of the inside of the back of the hood!

Motor yachts and motor sailers with enclosed steering positions enable a look-out to be kept in much greater comfort but the structure which provides the shelter creates its own blind arcs. These are particularly dangerous if the crew in the wheelhouse sit or stand in the same position for long periods. By doing so they run the risk of allowing another ship to approach on a steady bearing, and therefore a collision course, without being sighted.

To keep an effective look-out at night, *night vision* is needed. The human eye takes a considerable time to adapt to darkness after it has been exposed to white light. The actual time varies from one individual to another, but on average it takes about fifteen minutes, after exposure to white light of normal domestic intensity, before eyesight is fully effective in near darkness. To overcome this problem the accommodation and chart table should be lit by red lights at night. A red light does negligible damage to night vision and is much more restful to the eyes. Similarly, the use of searchlights and bright deck working lights should be kept to a minimum. Both are essential for certain operations, but a searchlight is particularly dangerous for two reasons. If it is inadvertently directed into another vessel's cockpit or wheelhouse it can cause sudden and unexpected night blindness to her crew. If its beam is relied on to pick up unlit navigational marks, the look-outs may see the marks which they are looking for quite clearly but, at the same time, fail to see other small boats or obstructions because their eyesight has been adversely affected by the use of the searchlight in the first place.

Smokers are always a potential hazard to night vision, the flare of a match or lighter being bright enough to cause loss of adaptation to anyone in the wheelhouse or cockpit who looks directly at it. If you smoke, warn the rest of the watch before you light up, and close one eye yourself to save its night-vision.

A good listening watch is particularly important in conditions of poor visibility. It is impossible to listen effectively from inside a closed wheelhouse and, in fog, at least one of the watch should be stationed on the open deck. In many sailing yachts the noise of the auxiliary engine is loud enough to mask any sounds from outboard. If this is the case the engines should be slowed or even stopped for two minutes in every five to allow an efficient listening watch to be kept.

Rule 6
Safe speed

Every vessel shall at all times proceed at a safe speed so that she can take proper and effective action to avoid collision and be stopped within a distance appropriate to the prevailing circumstance and conditions. In determining a safe speed the following factors shall be among those taken into account:

(a) By all vessels:

(i) the state of visibility;

(ii) the traffic density including concentrations of fishing vessels or any other vessels;

(iii) the manoeuvrability of the vessel with special reference to stopping distance and turning ability in the prevailing conditions;

(iv) at night the presence of background light such as from shore lights or from back scatter of her own lights;

(v) the state of wind, sea and current, and the proximity of navigational hazards;

(vi) the draught in relation to the available depth of water.

(b) Additionally, by vessels with operational radar:

(i) the characteristics, efficiency and limitations of the radar equipment;

(ii) any constraints imposed by the radar range scale in use;

(iii) the effect on radar detection of the sea state, weather and other sources of interference;

(iv) the possibility that small vessels, ice and other floating objects may not be detected by radar at an adequate range;

(v) the number, location and movement of vessels detected by radar;

(vi) the more exact assessment of the visibility that may be possible when radar is used to determine the range of vessels or other objects in the vicinity.

Note to Rule 6

Excessive speed is frequently found to be a contributory factor to collisions. Large ships, travelling fast, take a long time to stop and have a wide turning circle; high speeds reduce the amount of thinking time available to those in control. The second of these two speed problems is the most relevant to yachts.

A sailing yacht very seldom goes fast enough for her speed alone to contribute significantly to any risk of collision, but the manner in which she is being sailed, in order to achieve a relatively high speed, may well do so.

Consider the hypothetical case of a ketch sailing on a very broad reach at night. There are only two people in the watch on deck, and the rest of the crew are turned in below. On this point of sailing, she might be carrying a large headsail boomed out to windward, the main with a fore-guy on the main boom, a mizzen staysail and a mizzen. The time taken to prepare this rig for a large alteration of course could be as long as ten minutes. If unshipping the headsail boom and the fore-guy involve sending someone forward, it is certainly not likely to take less than five minutes.

The boat's speed would be reduced very little if course were altered to bring the wind further abeam so that the headsail could be set to leeward, and no speed would be lost by rigging the fore-guy through a block on the foredeck and back aft so that it could be released from the cockpit. Under this rig, course could be altered by one person in under thirty seconds.

A yacht, sailing at six knots, covers a mile in ten minutes and a ship steaming at twenty-four knots covers four miles in the same length of time. The skipper of our unhandy ketch meeting a fast container ship end on in a separation lane (where he has to give way) has therefore to decide that he must alter course when the ship is seven miles away, if he is to be able to make a substantial alteration before the range has closed to two miles. The yacht which is sailed short-handed under cumbersome rig is undoubtedly contravening the spirit, if not the letter of Rule 6.

For the motor yacht, which may be considerably faster than its sailing counterpart, speed through the water may be, in itself, a hazard. High traffic density, poor visibility and a background of shore lights can all contribute to confusion, which can only be increased by speed. It is impossible to be specific as to what is a safe speed, because the factors upon which it depends are so many and varied. Any skipper who is in any doubt as to whether or not he is going too fast, probably is!

Rule 7
Risk of collision

(a) Every vessel shall use all available means appropriate to the prevailing circumstances and conditions to determine if risk of collision exists. If there is any doubt such risk shall be deemed to exist.

(b) Proper use shall be made of radar equipment if fitted and operational, including long-range scanning to obtain early warning of risk of collision and radar plotting or equivalent systematic observation of detected objects.

(c) Assumptions shall not be made on the basis of scanty information, especially scanty radar information.

(d) In determining if risk of collision exists the following considerations shall be among those taken into account:

(i) such risk shall be deemed to exist if the compass bearing of an approaching vessel does not appreciably change;

(ii) such risk may sometimes exist even when an appreciable bearing change is evident, particularly when approaching a very large vessel or a tow or when approaching a vessel at close range.

Note to Rule 7

This is the first Rule which is directly concerned with collision avoidance. Whenever a situation arises in which two ships approach, the master of each has to answer two questions. Is there a risk of collision in this situation? If so, what action should I take to avoid it? This Rule gives guidelines on answering the first question.

Any collision situation poses a problem of relative velocities. If the relative movement of the two ships is directly towards each other then, unless one of them alters course, they will collide. This situation is easily identified because when it exists the compass bearing of one ship from the other remains steady. A typical collision situation is shown in *Fig 1*. The compass bearing of ship B from ship A remains steady at 045° as they close. In this particular case, the relative bearing of B from A also remains on a steady course. If, in this situation, A had

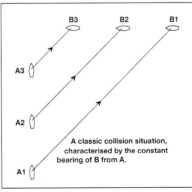

A classic collision situation, characterised by the constant bearing of B from A.

Fig 1

been steered erratically, yawing 10° either side of her mean course, the relative bearing of B would have altered through 20° as she closed. The compass bearing, however, would have altered very little and the collision would still have happened.

Fig 2 shows a situation in which there is a much more dramatic change in the relative bearing of B from A. Between positions A1 and A2, B is some 50° abaft A's beam. A then alters course about 90° to starboard so that, when she reaches position A3, B is some 40° forward of her beam. Continuing to position A4, however, it becomes apparent that although there has been a radical alteration of course, and consequent change of relative bearing, there has been no change of compass bearings and the two ships are still on a collision course.

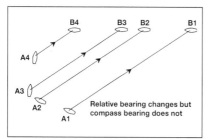

Fig 2

Upon looking at these two situations, it becomes clear that the automatic reaction, on sighting another vessel at sea, should be to take a compass bearing of her and a second bearing a few minutes later. If there has been no appreciable change and the range is decreasing then a collision situation exists. Modern, very small, hand bearing compasses (which can be worn on a lanyard round the neck) simplify the practical aspects of taking quick bearings from the cockpit or wheelhouse. Alternatively, it is possible to check for a steady bearing situation by lining the other ship up with a stanchion or other deck fitting, checking each time before doing so that the yacht is on the same course and the head is in exactly the same attitude for each sighting. The snag with this method is that if any alteration of course has to be made, the whole process has to start again

from scratch, using a different deck fitting or stanchion.

With experience, a potentially dangerous situation can often be recognised from the relative bearing and aspect of the other ship. The danger of relying on a 'by eye' assessment of collision risk is that even the most experienced seaman can be misled. Although a background of seagoing experience is a great help, only the foolhardy dispense completely with compass bearings in assessing risk of collision.

Rule 8
Action to avoid collision

(a) Any action taken to avoid collision shall, if the circumstances of the case admit, be positive, made in ample time and with due regard to the observance of good seamanship.

(b) Any alteration of course and/or speed to avoid collision shall, if the circumstances of the case admit, be large enough to be readily apparent to another vessel observing visually or by radar; a succession of small alterations of course and/or speed should be avoided.

(c) If there is sufficient sea room, alteration of course alone may be the most effective action to avoid a close-quarters situation provided that it is made in good time, is substantial and does not result in another close-quarters situation.

(d) Action taken to avoid collision with another vessel shall be such as to result in passing at a safe distance. The effectiveness of the action shall be carefully checked until the other vessel is finally past and clear.

(e) If necessary to avoid collision or allow more time to assess the situation, a vessel shall slacken her speed or take all way off by stopping or reversing her means of propulsion.

(f) (i) A vessel which, by any of these rules, is required not to impede the passage or safe passage of another vessel shall, when required by the circumstances of the case, take early action to allow sufficient sea room for the safe passage of the other vessel.

(ii) A vessel required not to impede the passage or safe passage of another vessel is not relieved of this obligation if approaching the other vessel so as to involve risk of collision and shall, when taking action, have full regard to the action which may be required by the rules of this part.

(iii) A vessel the passage of which is not to be impeded remains fully obliged to comply with the rules of this part when the two vessels are approaching one another so as to involve risk of collision.

Note to Rule 8

This regulation answers the second of our basic questions: "What action should I take to avoid a collision?" There are five criteria to be taken into account when finding an answer to this question.

1 Make the alteration early enough so that there is no possibility of doubt that you are going to take avoiding action well before a close-quarters situation develops.

2 Make a large enough alteration of course for your intentions to be absolutely clear.

3 Avoid crossing ahead of the ship to which you are giving way.

4 Take care that in altering course to avoid one ship you are not increasing the risk of collision with another.

5 Consider all the navigational implications of the situation. In confined waters, when giving way to a large ship, the most sensible alteration of course to make is frequently one which takes the small craft out of the buoyed channel.

For an alteration of course to be absolutely obvious, particularly at night, it should involve presenting a totally different *aspect* to the other ship. In *Fig 3(a)* the alteration between A1 and A2 is probably sufficient to avoid a collision but, throughout the manoeuvre, A continues to present her starboard bow, or by night her starboard side light, to B. In *Fig 3(b)*, however, the alteration between A1 and A2 is large

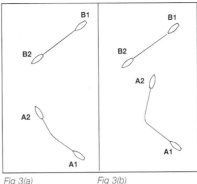

Fig 3(a)　　　　　　Fig 3(b)

enough to present a totally different "aspect" and it is abundantly clear to B that A has altered course to pass under her stern.

When two ships meet almost end-on, there is frequently a temptation to make a small alteration of course to avoid crossing ahead. *Fig 4* illustrates the inherent danger in this sort of manoeuvre and why it should be avoided. At position 1, A sights B fine on her port bow, on a near reciprocal course and wrongly decides that a small alteration to port will avoid trouble and a *crossing ahead* situation. Moving on to position 2, A has made her course alteration but B has decided almost simultaneously to make a small alteration to starboard which would clear a potentially dangerous situation. The scene is now set for a slapstick comedy (or tragedy) of the two men meeting in doorway variety, but the ending will be a very serious matter.

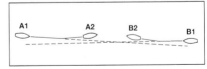

Fig 4

The case described above is doubly dangerous if the ships involved are not actually in sight of each other but are working on radar information. These are the opening moves in a classic *radar assisted collision*.

Alterations of speed are very seldom immediately apparent to another ship, and the only useful speed alteration is a drastic reduction. This can frequently give much needed additional time to resolve a complex situation. An even more effective manoeuvre in a complicated multi-ship situation, or when confronted by a ship which will not acknowledge its responsibility to give way, is the 180° turn. This will nearly always allow the confusion to clear.

Paragraph (f) is intended to clarify the difference between the terms *Shall keep out of the way of* and *Shall not impede.* Sub-sections (i) and (iii) are entirely logical. Sub-section (ii) is more contentious and introduces scope for doubt in a closing situation between two vessels as the close-quarters phase of the encounter is reached. The final sentence of this paragraph is particularly important, as a vessel which is taking action *not to impede,* must anticipate the most likely action of a vessel which is directed to *keep out of the way of.*

A typical instance to which this Rule would apply is illustrated in *Fig 4(a).* A is a large vessel, following a separation lane, B is a small vessel crossing the lane. The skipper of B is uncertain whether or not A will hold her course or take action to avoid collision. If A does take avoiding action she is most likely to do so by a turn to starboard. Thus it would be dangerous for B to alter course to port, the safest manoeuvre is for her to turn 90° to starboard, which should allow for A either to hold her course or to turn to starboard.

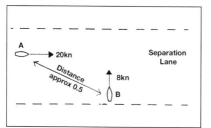

Fig 4 (a)

Rule 9
Narrow channels

(a) A vessel proceeding along the course of a narrow channel or fairway shall keep as near to the outer limit of the channel or fairway which lies on her starboard side as is safe and practicable.

(b) A vessel of less than 20 metres in length or a sailing vessel shall not impede the passage of a vessel which can safely navigate only within a narrow channel or fairway.

(c) A vessel engaged in fishing shall not impede the passage of any other vessel navigating within a narrow channel or fairway.

(d) A vessel shall not cross a narrow channel or fairway if such crossing impedes the passage of a vessel which can safely navigate only within such channel or fairway. The latter vessel may use the sound signal prescribed in Rule 34(d) if in doubt as to the intention of the crossing vessel.

(e) (i) In a narrow channel or fairway when overtaking can take place only if the vessel to be overtaken has to take action to permit safe passing, the vessel intending to overtake shall indicate her intention by sounding the appropriate signal prescribed in Rule 34(c)(i). The vessel to be overtaken shall, if in agreement, sound the appropriate signal prescribed in Rule 34(c)(ii) and take steps to permit safe passing. If in doubt she may sound the signals prescribed in Rule 34(d).

(ii) This Rule does not relieve the overtaking vessel of her obligation under Rule 13.

(f) A vessel nearing a bend or an area of a narrow channel or fairway where other vessels may be obscured by an intervening obstruction shall navigate with particular alertness and caution and shall sound the appropriate signal prescribed in Rule 34(e).

(g) Any vessel shall, if the circumstances of the case admit, avoid anchoring in a narrow channel.

Note to Rule 9

A narrow channel is not defined, for the very good reason that the term is a relative one.

The ability to apply this Rule calls for a certain amount of background knowledge of ship types and handling characteristics. In general, however, it should be assumed that any channel which is marked by port and starboard hand buoys will be treated as a narrow channel by ocean-going ships. Thus, the Thames Estuary inward of the Edinburgh Channels, and the Solent between the Needles Fairway and the Nab Tower, are narrow channels as far as deep draught ships are concerned.

Once a ship is committed to a narrow channel, in the approaches to a harbour, it has to be manoeuvred with precision. If it has to slow down, it may lose steerage way and if it deviates from its planned track it may not be able to turn tightly enough in the next bend. Any yachtsman who impedes the progress of a large ship in a narrow channel is, therefore, being totally irresponsible. Note that Rule 9(b) is mandatory - *shall not* are the words used.

Rule 10
Traffic separation schemes

(a) This rule applies to traffic separation schemes adopted by the Organization and does not relieve any vessel of her obligation under any other rule.

(b) A vessel using a traffic separation scheme shall:

(i) proceed in the appropriate traffic lane in the general direction of traffic flow for that lane;

(ii) so far as practicable keep clear of a traffic separation line or separation zone;

(iii) normally join or leave a traffic lane at the termination of the lane, but when joining or leaving from either side shall do so at as small an angle to the general direction of traffic flow as practicable.

(c) A vessel shall, so far as practicable, avoid crossing traffic lanes, but if obliged to do so shall cross on a heading as nearly as practicable at right angles to the general direction of traffic flow.

(d) (i) A vessel shall not use an inshore traffic zone when she can safely use the appropiate traffic lane within the adjacent traffic separation scheme. However, vessels of less than 20 metres in length, sailing vessels and vessels engaged in fishing may use the inshore traffic zone.

(ii) Notwithstanding sub-paragraph (d)(i) a vessel may use an inshore traffic zone when en route to or from a port, offshore installation or structure, pilot station or any other place situated within a traffic zone, or to avoid immediate danger.

(e) A vessel other than a crossing vessel or a vessel joining or leaving a lane shall not normally enter a separation zone or cross a separation line except:

(i) in case of emergency to avoid immediate danger;

(ii) to engage in fishing within a separation zone.

(f) A vessel navigating in areas near the terminations of traffic separation schemes shall do so with particular caution.

(g) A vessel shall so far as practicable avoid anchoring in a traffic separation scheme or in areas near its terminations.

(h) A vessel not using a traffic separation scheme shall avoid it by as wide a margin as is practicable.

(i) A vessel engaged in fishing shall not impede the passage of any vessel following a traffic lane.

(j) A vessel of less than 20 metres in length or a sailing vessel shall not impede the safe passage of a power-driven vessel following a traffic lane.

(k) A vessel restricted in her ability to manoeuvre when engaged in an operation for the maintenance of safety of navigation in a traffic separation scheme is exempted from complying with this Rule to the extent necessary to carry out the operation.

(l) A vessel restricted in her ability to manoeuvre when engaged in an operation for the laying, servicing or picking up of a submarine cable, within a traffic separation scheme, is exempted from complying with this Rule to the extent necessary to carry out the operation.

Note to Rule 10

The locations of all traffic separation schemes are marked on Admiralty Charts. Schemes have been introduced in areas where there is congestion in an attempt to separate the shipping into identifiable one-way lanes. Each scheme consists of two lanes separated by a separation zone and ships using the scheme are required to navigate in the proper lane.

Yachtsmen should especially note Rule 10(c) and 10(j).

Rule 10(c) is intended to encourage vessels crossing separation lanes to do so as quickly as possible so it would be in contravention of the spirit of this Rule for a sailing boat to remain becalmed in a lane. If the speed drops below about 3 knots it is time to start the engine and motor clear.

Rule 10(c) applies to the general route to be taken by a vessel crossing a traffic lane, it imposes no restriction on action which may be taken to avoid a collision.

A sailing vessel crossing traffic lanes against a head-wind might be well advised to consider motoring. However, if that is impractical she is not infringing the Rule by steering a close-hauled course on the tack which makes her heading as close as possible to a right-angle to the direction of traffic flow.

Note that it is the heading, not the ground track which must be at right angles. In *Fig 4(b)* B is on the correct heading for crossing a lane; A, although following a ground track at right angles to the lane, is not heading at right angles and is therefore on an incorrect course.

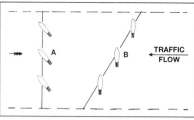

Fig 4 (b)

A's course made good is at right angles to the traffic flow and she presents a quarter aspect to ships following the lane.

B's heading is at right angles to the traffic flow and she presents a true 90° crossing aspect to ships following the lane. B's time of crossing is shorter than A's.

Rule 10(j) is amplified by Rule 8(f).

SECTION II
Conduct of vessels in sight of one another
Rule 11
Application

Rules in this Section apply to vessels in sight of one another.

Note to Rule 11

The purpose of this seemingly naive and obvious Rule is to make it quite clear that the Rules in this section are not intended to apply when the ships involved can observe each other only on radar.

Rule 12
Sailing vessels

(a) When two sailing vessels are approaching one another, so as to involve risk of collision, one of them shall keep out of the way of the other as follows:

    (i) when each has the wind on a different side, the vessel which has the wind on the port side shall keep out of the way of the other;

    (ii) when both have the wind on the same side, the vessel which is to windward shall keep out of the way of the vessel which is to leeward;

(iii) if a vessel with the wind on the port side sees a vessel to windward and cannot determine with certainty whether the other vessel has the wind on the port or on the starboard side, she shall keep out of the way of the other.

(b) For the purposes of this Rule the windward side shall be deemed to be the side opposite to that on which the mainsail is carried or, in the case of a square-rigged vessel, the side opposite to that on which the largest fore-and-aft sail is carried.

Note to Rule 12

This Rule is illustrated in *Fig 5*.

Rule 12(a)(iii), resolves the difficult situation where a yacht, close-hauled on the port tack encounters another yacht which is running free.

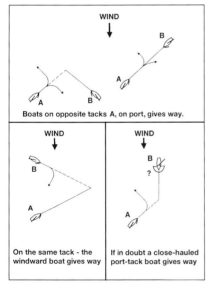

Fig 5

It is often extremely difficult, and by night impossible, for the close-hauled yacht to determine upon which tack the approach yacht is sailing. In case of doubt, the onus is firmly placed upon the close-hauled yacht to assume that she must give way and do so.

Rule 13
Overtaking

(a) Notwithstanding anything contained in the Rules of Part B, Sections I and II any vessel overtaking any other shall keep out of the way of the vessel being overtaken.

(b) A vessel shall be deemed to be overtaking when coming up with another vessel from a direction more than 22.5 degrees abaft her beam, that is, in such a position with reference to the vessel she is overtaking, that at night she would be able to see only the sternlight of that vessel but neither of her sidelights.

(c) When a vessel is in any doubt as to whether she is overtaking another, she shall assume that this is the case and act accordingly.

(d) Any subsequent alteration of the bearing between the two vessels shall not make the overtaking vessel a crossing vessel within the meaning of these Rules or relieve her of the duty of keeping clear of the overtaken vessel until she is finally past and clear.

Note to Rule 13

Paragraph (a) of this Rule spells out its priority over other steering and sailing Rules.

Furthermore, it applies equally to sailing and power-driven vessels.

Paragraph (d) places the onus on the overtaking vessel to keep clear if she initially approaches from more than 22.5° abaft the beam, no matter what the relative bearing between the two vessels may subsequently become. It does NOT, however, imply that the vessel being overtaken is free to alter course across the bows of the vessel overtaking it. Such action would be an obvious contradiction of good seamanship but unfortunately happens, largely because it is difficult to see aft from the bridges of some ships and the natural tendency is to concentrate on looking out ahead.

To avoid embarrassing an overtaking vessel, or any other vessel for that matter, there is a simple routine when altering course which should be followed before putting the helm over. Look astern, over both quarters, to make sure that nothing is overtaking. Then look along the bearing of the new course and consider what effect the alteration is going to have on any other vessel in the vicinity. If the new course is likely to give rise to a situation in which there will be risk of collision, modify the navigational plan, either by slowing down or by altering to a different course.

The overtaking sector is illustrated in *Fig 6*.

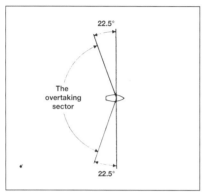

Fig 6

Rule 14
Head-on situation

(a) When two power-driven vessels are meeting on reciprocal or nearly reciprocal courses so as to involve risk of collision each shall alter her course to starboard so that each shall pass on the port side of the other.

(b) Such a situation shall be deemed to exist when a vessel sees the other ahead or nearly ahead and by night she could see the masthead lights of the other in a line or nearly in a line and/or both sidelights and by day she observes the corresponding aspect of the other vessel.

(c) When a vessel is in any doubt as to whether such a situation exists she shall assume that it does exist and act accordingly.

Note to Rule 14

This perfectly simple Rule is one which, surprisingly, causes problems. *Fig 7* shows the correct action to take in an end-on situation. Both vessels alter course to starboard and pass port side to port side. The difficulties occur with a situation such as that illustrated in *Fig 8*.

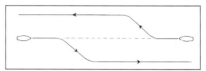

Fig 7

Fig 8

The two ships are meeting *on reciprocal or nearly reciprocal courses* and if both maintain their course there <u>will</u> be no collision, but they will pass dangerously close down each other's starboard sides. If either of them alters course to starboard, as the Rule requires, she will be crossing ahead of the other and there is a natural reluctance to do this. A seemingly attractive alternative is a very small alteration of course to port which, it is hoped, will increase the passing distance to make it acceptably safe, but this would be a fatal mistake. If A, wrongly, alters course 10° to port and at the same instant B, correctly, alters course 15° to starboard we are faced with our two men meeting in doorway slapstick comedy. The only really safe course of action for B to take, if A has made this initial mistake, is to reverse course or to stop. If B tries to guess whether A's next move will be to compound his error and alter another 10° to port, or to realise that his initial move was wrong and turn back to starboard, he stands a one-in-two chance of guessing wrong. A one-in-two chance of a collision is just not good enough and B will be foolhardy if he allows this potentially calamitous situation to develop any further by continuing to close the range.

Rule 15
Crossing situation

When two power-driven vessels are crossing so as to involve risk of collision, the vessel which has the other on her own starboard side shall keep out of the way and shall, it the circumstances of the case admit, avoid crossing ahead of the other vessel.

Note to Rule 15

This Rule is illustrated in *Fig 9*. In 99% of crossing situations the correct action for the giving-way vessel to take is to alter course to starboard. Occasionally the presence of another ship, or a navigational hazard, will prevent this and it is possible that situations might arise in which the giving-way vessel should alter to port.

If an alteration to port is made, it is likely to result in crossing ahead of the stand-on vessel. Therefore, it must be a very substantial alteration.

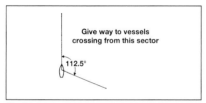

Give way to vessels crossing from this sector

112.5°

Fig 9

Rule 16
Action by give-way vessel

Every vessel which is directed to keep out of the way of another vessel shall, so far as possible, take early and substantial action to keep well clear.

Note to Rule 16

This is an important re-statement of Rule 8(a).

Rule 17
Action by stand-on vessel

(a) (i) Where one of two vessels is to keep out of the way the other shall keep her course and speed.

(ii) The latter vessel may however take action to avoid collision by her manoeuvre alone, as soon as it becomes apparent to her that the vessel required to keep out of the way is not taking appropriate action in compliance with these Rules.

(b) When, from any cause, the vessel required to keep her course and speed finds herself so close that collision cannot be avoided by the action of the give-way vessel alone, she shall take such action as will best aid to avoid collision.

(c) A power-driven vessel which takes action in a crossing situation in accordance with sub-paragraph (a)(ii) of this Rule to avoid collision with another power-driven vessel shall, if the circumstances of the case admit, not alter course to port for a vessel on her own port side.

(d) This Rule does not relieve the give-way vessel of her obligation to keep out of the way.

Note to Rule 17

This Rule causes more heart-searching than any other. Paragraph (a)(i) *requires* the vessel having right-of-way to maintain her course and speed. Paragraph (a)(ii) *allows* her to take avoiding action as soon as it becomes apparent that the giving-way vessel is not meeting her obligation to keep clear. Paragraph (b) *requires* that she should not be involved in a collision.

Paragraph (a)(ii) is the key. It gives the stand-on vessel the option of taking avoiding action as soon as it is apparent that the give-way vessel is not acting in accordance with the Rules and, according to Rule 16, action to avoid collision should be *early*. The stand-on vessel is not, therefore, bound to hang grimly on in a trial of nerve.

The small craft skipper is in a particularly difficult situation when meeting a large ship at night. He may well have right-of-way according to the Rules, but there are special circumstances to be taken into account. A yacht is relatively small and its navigation lights are, by comparison with the white masthead lights of a merchant ship, extremely dim. Even in daylight, a yacht with white sails and a white hull is extremely difficult to spot against a background of white wave crests. It is not suggested that yachts should always keep clear of large ships, but the yachtsman must be aware that he may not be spotted by the officer of the watch of a ship until the time for *early* action is past, and must be ready to take action to avoid a close quarters situation. Waiting until a collision cannot be averted by the action of one vessel alone is more than merely unseamanlike! In a confrontation between a yacht and a supertanker it is lunacy!

Whenever a stand-on vessel alters course to avoid collision it must be remembered that the other ship may alter simultaneously. Hence the warning in Rule 17(c) against an alteration of course to port in a crossing situation. The give-way ship may well alter course late, and in doing so she will probably alter to starboard to fulfil her obligation to avoid crossing ahead.

The safest course of action for a stand-on vessel which is obliged to alter course to avoid collision is to turn directly away from the other ship. This manoeuvre has the advantages of reducing the relative rate of closing and of presenting the smallest possible target. It is not the perfect solution to this difficult problem, just the least unsatisfactory answer to a highly unsatisfactory question.

Rule 18
Responsibilities between vessels

Except where Rules 9, 10 and 13 otherwise require:

(a) A power-driven vessel underway shall keep out of the way of:
  (i) a vessel not under command;
  (ii) a vessel restricted in her ability to manoeuvre;
  (iii) a vessel engaged in fishing;
  (iv) a sailing vessel;

(b) A sailing vessel underway shall keep out of the way of:
  (i) a vessel not under command;
  (ii) a vessel restricted in her ability to manoeuvre;

(iii) a vessel engaged in fishing.

(c) A vessel engaged in fishing when underway shall as far as possible, keep out of the way of:
  (i) a vessel not under command;
  (ii) a vessel restricted in her ability to manoeuvre.

(d) (i) Any vessel other than a vessel not under command or a vessel restricted in her ability to manoeuvre shall, if the circumstances of the case admit, avoid impeding the safe passage of a vessel constrained by her draught, exhibiting the signals in Rule 28;

  (ii) A vessel constrained by her draught shall navigate with particular caution having full regard to her special condition.

(e) A seaplane on the water shall, in general, keep well clear of all vessels and avoid impeding their navigation. In circumstances, however, where risk of collision exists, she shall comply with the Rules of this Part.

Note to Rule 18

Except in narrow channels traffic separation schemes and overtaking situations, this Rule establishes a list of priorities according to manoeuvrability. It is a very logical Rule, asking that the more manoeuvrable should give way to the less manoeuvrable.

SECTION III
Conduct of vessels in restricted visibility
Rule 19
Conduct of vessels in restricted visibility

(a) This Rule applies to vessels not in sight of one another when navigating in or near an area of restricted visibility.

(b) Every vessel shall proceed at a safe speed adapted to the prevailing circumstances and conditions of restricted visibility. A power-driven vessel shall have her engines ready for immediate manoeuvre.

(c) Every vessel shall have due regard to the prevailing circumstances and conditions of restricted visibility when complying with the Rules of Section I of this Part.

(d) A vessel which detects by radar alone the presence of another vessel shall determine if a close-quarters situation is developing and/or risk of collision exists. If so, she shall take avoiding action in ample time, provided that when such action consists of an alteration of course, so far as possible the following shall be avoided:

(i) an alteration of course to port for a vessel forward of the beam, other than for a vessel being overtaken;

(ii) an alteration of course towards a vessel abeam or abaft the beam.

(e) Except where it has been determined that a risk of collision does not exist, every vessel which hears apparently forward of her beam the fog signal of another vessel, or which cannot avoid a close-quarters situation with another vessel forward of her beam, shall reduce her speed to the minimum at which she can be kept on her course. She shall if necessary take all her way off and in any event navigate with extreme caution until danger of collision is over.

Note to Rule 19

Fog at sea considerably increases the risk of collision. Radar has made it possible for a skilled operator to navigate a ship through fog with safety but it is by no means a panacea for all poor visibility problems. A misinterpreted radar picture can cause a collision, a collision which might never have happened if radar had not been used. There are four things which a yachtsman can do to reduce the risk of being run down in fog:

• Use a radar reflector.

• Keep a good lookout by both sight and sound.

• Be ready to take immediate and drastic avoiding action.

• Keep clear of shipping channels.

An efficient radar reflector greatly increases the probability of a yacht being detected on radar. The design of radar reflectors has improved considerably in recent years and several are now available which have very good performance characteristics and are relatively easy to rig permanently aloft.

The traditional, octohedral type of reflector is relatively inexpensive and can give good results, provided that it is correctly mounted.

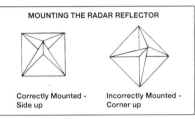

MOUNTING THE RADAR REFLECTOR

Correctly Mounted - Side up

Incorrectly Mounted - Corner up

Fig 10

In general, the larger the reflector the more effective it is likely to be. Reflectors smaller than the 50cm size are unlikely to be very much use and even the smallest yachts should use one of this size. The higher the reflector is mounted, the more effective it will be and it should certainly be at least four metres above the waterline.

One of the easiest places to fit a radar reflector is at the masthead. It is out of the way of the sails and running rigging. The snag is, it becomes difficult to have a burgee, a masthead light and an anemometer there as well. In yachts with twin backstays, it is often possible to fit the reflector between the stays on a wooden or metal spreader. This overcomes the problem of overcrowding at the masthead and makes it easier to mount it correctly.

Another answer, particularly favoured by racing yachts in which the windage of a permanently mounted reflector is unacceptable, is to hoist it to the crosstrees on a flag halyard, but the chafe caused by a sizeable lump of metal swinging about on a halyard is considerable and it is difficult to mount the reflector properly. In yachts which do not race too seriously the permanent fitting has the great advantage that the reflector is always there when it is needed. It is an awkward shape to stow when assembled and if it is lowered and folded in times of good visibility, it may not be available at the crucial moment when visibility suddenly decreases.

Keeping a good lookout in fog depends upon using ears as well as eyes. In a motor yacht with an auxiliary engine running, this will probably entail sending someone forward, not so much because they will see more from the bows but because they will be able to hear more if they are as far as possible from the noise of the engine.

Fog is often accompanied by a calm. This makes sailing yachts particularly vulnerable because, even if they do hear an approaching vessel and decide that a collision is imminent, they can do nothing about getting out of the way if they do not have steerage way. For this reason, the engine should always be ready for starting when the fog and calm happen together. To have the engine ticking over may be necessary (if it is one which is temperamental about starting) but this is to a certain extent self-defeating, because the noise it makes may prevent the watch on deck from hearing anything else.

When fog is accompanied by a good sailing breeze, care has to be taken to make sure that the boat can manoeuvre quickly. Spinnakers and boomed-out headsails are unseamanlike sails in fog.

In poor visibility, a busy shipping lane is no place for a yacht. The comparatively shallow draught of most yachts often allows them to take refuge from larger ships by standing into shallow water. Areas such as the Thames Estuary and the Solent lend themselves particularly well to this tactic. A yacht in twelve feet of water or less is absolutely safe from risk of collision with a merchant ship of any size, and in thick fog the only really safe course of action is to head for shallow water and anchor.

PART C LIGHTS AND SHAPES

Rule 20
Application

(a) Rules in this part shall be complied with in all weathers.

(b) The Rules concerning lights shall be complied with from sunset to sunrise, and during such times no other lights shall be exhibited, except such lights as cannot be mistaken for the lights specified in these Rules or do not impair their visibility or distinctive character, or interfere with the keeping of a proper look-out.

(c) The lights prescribed by these Rules shall, if carried, also be exhibited from sunrise to sunset in restricted visibility and may be exhibited in all other circumstances when it is deemed necessary.

(d) The Rules concerning shapes shall be complied with by day.

(e) The lights and shapes specified in these Rules shall comply with the provisions of Annex I to these regulations.

Rule 21
Definitions

(a) *Masthead light* means a white light placed over the fore and aft centreline of the vessel showing an unbroken light over an arc of the horizon of 225 degrees and so fixed as to show the light from right ahead to 22.5 degrees abaft the beam on either side of the vessel.

(b) *Sidelights* means a green light on the starboard side and a red light on the port side each showing an unbroken light over an arc of the horizon of 112.5 degrees and so fixed as to show the light from right ahead to 22.5 degrees abaft the beam on its respective side. In a vessel of less than 20 metres in length the sidelights may be combined in one lantern carried on the fore and aft centre-line of the vessel.

(c) *Sternlight* means a white light placed as nearly as practicable at the stem showing an unbroken light over an arc of the horizon of 135 degrees and so fixed as to show the light 67.5 degrees from right aft on each side of the vessel.

(d) *Towing light* means a yellow light having the same characteristics as the *sternlight* defined in paragraph (c) of this Rule.

(e) *All round light* means a light showing an unbroken light over an arc of the horizon of 360 degrees.

(f) *Flashing light* means a light flashing at regular intervals at a frequency of 120 flashes or more per minute.

Rule 22
Visibility of lights

The lights prescribed in these Rules shall have an intensity as specified in Section 8 of Annex I to these regulations so as to be visible at the following minimum ranges:

(a) In vessels of 50 metres or more in length:
- a masthead light, 6 miles;
- a sidelight, 3 miles;
- a sternlight, 3 miles;
- a towing light, 3 miles;
- a white, red, green or yellow all-round light, 3 miles.

(b) In vessels of 12 metres or more in length but less than 50 metres in length:
- a masthead light, 5 miles; except that where the length of the vessel is less than 20 metres, 3 miles;
- a sidelight, 2 miles;
- a sternlight, 2 miles;
- a towing light, 2 miles;
- a white, red, green or yellow all-round light, 2 miles.

(c) In vessels of less than 12 metres in length:
- a masthead light, 2 miles;
- a sidelight, 1 mile;
- a sternlight, 2 miles;
- a towing light, 2 miles;
- a white, red, green or yellow all-round light, 2 miles.

(d) In inconspicuous, partly submerged vessels or objects being towed:
- a white all-round light, 3 miles.

Note to Rule 22

The requirements for visibility are clearly defined and should be noted.

Rule 23
Power-driven vessels underway

(a) A power-driven vessel underway shall exhibit:
(i) a masthead light forward;
(ii) a second masthead light abaft of and higher than the forward one; except that a vessel of less than 50 metres in length shall not be obliged to exhibit such light but may do so;
(iii) sidelights;
(iv) a sternlight.

(b) An air-cushion vessel when operating in the non-displacement mode shall, in addition to the lights prescribed in paragraph (a) of this Rule exhibit an all-round flashing yellow light.

(c) (i) A power-driven vessel of less than 12 metres in length may in lieu of the lights prescribed in paragraph (a) of this Rule exhibit an all-round white light and sidelights;
(ii) a power-driven vessel of less than 7 metres in length whose maximum speed does not exceed 7 knots may in lieu of the lights prescribed in paragraph (a) of this Rule exhibit an all-round white light and shall, if practicable, also exhibit sidelights;
(iii) the masthead light or all-round white light on a power-driven vessel of less than 12 metres in length may be displaced from the fore and aft centreline of the vessel if centreline fitting is not practicable, provided that the sidelights are combined in one lantern which shall be carried on the fore and aft centreline of the vessel or located as nearly as practicable in the same fore and aft line as the masthead light or the all-round white light.

Rule 24
Towing and pushing

(a) A power-driven vessel when towing shall exhibit:
(i) instead of the light prescribed in Rule 23(a)(i) or (ii), two masthead lights in a vertical line. When the length of the tow, measuring from the stern of the towing vessel to the after end of the tow exceeds 200 metres, three such lights in a vertical line;
(ii) sidelights;
(iii) a sternlight;
(iv) a towing light in a vertical line above the sternlight;
(v) when the length of the tow exceeds 200 metres, a diamond shape where it can best be seen.

(b) When a pushing vessel and a vessel being pushed ahead are rigidly connected in a composite unit they shall be regarded as a power-driven vessel and exhibit the light prescribed in Rule 23.

(c) A power-driven vessel when pushing ahead or towing alongside, except in the case of a composite unit, shall exhibit:
(i) instead of the light prescribed in Rule 23(a)(i) or (ii), two masthead lights in a vertical line;
(ii) sidelights;
(iii) a sternlight.

(d) A power-driven vessel to which paragraph (a) or (c) of this Rule applies shall also comply with Rule 23(a)(ii).

(e) A vessel or object being towed, other than those mentioned in paragraph (g) of the Rule, shall exhibit:
(i) sidelights;

(ii) a sternlight;

(iii) when the length of the tow exceeds 200 metres, a diamond shape where it can best be seen.

(f) Provided that any number of vessels being towed alongside or pushed in a group shall be lighted as one vessel,

(i) a vessel being pushed ahead, not being part of a composite unit, shall exhibit at the forward end, sidelights;

(ii) a vessel being towed alongside shall exhibit a sternlight and at the forward end, sidelights.

(g) An inconspicuous, partly submerged vessel or object, or combination of such vessels or objects being towed, shall exhibit:

(i) if it is less than 25 metres in breadth, one all-round white light at or near the forward end and one at or near the after end except that dracones need not exhibit a light at or near the forward end;

(ii) if it is 25 metres or more in breadth, two additional all-round white lights at or near the extremities of its breadth;

(iii) if it exceeds 100 metres in length, additional all-round white lights between the lights prescribed in sub-paragraphs (i) and (ii) so that the distance between the lights shall not exceed 100 metres;

(iv) a diamond shape at or near the aftermost extremity of the last vessel or object being towed and if the length of the tow exceeds 200 metres an additional diamond shape where it can best be seen and located as far forward as is practicable.

(h) Where from any sufficient cause it is impracticable for a vessel or object being towed to exhibit the lights or shapes prescribed in paragraph (e) or (g) of this Rule, all possible measures shall be taken to light the vessel or object towed or at least to indicate the

presence of such vessel or object.

(i) Where from any sufficient cause it is impracticable for a vessel not normally engaged in towing operations to display the lights prescribed in paragraph (a) or (c) of this Rule, such vessel shall not be required to exhibit those lights when engaged in towing another vessel in distress or otherwise in need of assistance. All possible measures shall be taken to indicate the nature of the relationship between the towing vessel and the vessel being towed as authorized by Rule 36, in particular by illuminating the towline.

Rule 25
Sailing vessels underway and vessels under oars

(a) A sailing vessel underway shall exhibit:

(i) sidelights;

(ii) a sternlight.

(b) In a sailing vessel of less than 20 metres in length the lights prescribed in paragraph (a) of this Rule may be combined in one lantern carried at or near the top of the mast where it can best be seen.

(c) A sailing vessel underway may, in addition to the lights prescribed in paragraph (a) of this Rule, exhibit at or near the top of the mast, where they can best be seen, two all-round lights in a vertical line, the upper being red and the lower green, but these lights shall not be exhibited in conjunction with the combined lantern permitted by paragraph (b) of this Rule.

(d) (i) A sailing vessel of less than 7 metres in length shall, if practicable, exhibit the lights prescribed in paragraph (a) or (b) of this Rule, but if she does not, she shall have ready at hand an electric torch or lighted lantern showing a white light which shall be exhibited in sufficient time to prevent collision.

(ii) A vessel under oars may exhibit the lights prescribed in this Rule for sailing vessels, but if she does not, she shall have ready at hand an electric torch or lighted lantern showing a white light which shall be exhibited in sufficient time to prevent collision.

(e) A vessel proceeding under sail when also being propelled by machinery shall exhibit forward where it can best be seen a conical shape, apex downwards.

Rule 26
Fishing vessels

(a) A vessel engaged in fishing, whether underway or at anchor, shall exhibit only the lights and shapes prescribed in this Rule.

(b) A vessel when engaged in trawling, by which is meant the dragging through the water of a dredge net or other apparatus used as a fishing appliance, shall exhibit:

(i) two all-round lights in a vertical line, the upper being green and the lower white, or a shape consisting of two cones with their apexes together in a vertical line one above the other;

(ii) a masthead light abaft of and higher than the all-round green light; a vessel of less than 50 metres in length shall not be obliged to exhibit such a light but may do so;

(iii) when making way through the water, in addition to the lights prescribed in this paragraph, sidelights and a sternlight.

(c) A vessel engaged in fishing, other than trawling, shall exhibit:

(i) two all-round lights in a vertical line, the upper being red and the lower white, or a shape consisting of two cones with apexes together in a line one above the other;

(ii) when there is outlying gear extending more than 150 metres horizontally from the vessel, an all-round white light or a cone apex upwards in the direction of the gear;

(iii) when making way through the water, in addition to the lights prescribed in this paragraph, sidelights and a sternlight.

(d) The additional signals described in Annex II to these regulations apply to a vessel engaged in fishing in close proximity to other vessels engaged in fishing.

(e) A vessel when not engaged in fishing shall not exhibit the lights or shapes prescribed in this Rule, but only those prescribed for a vessel of her length.

Rule 27
Vessels not under command or restricted in their ability to manoeuvre

(a) A vessel not under command shall exhibit.

(i) two all-round red lights in a vertical line where they can best be seen;

(ii) two balls or similar shapes in a vertical line where they can best be seen;

(iii) when making way through the water, in addition to the lights prescribed in this paragraph, sidelights and a sternlight.

(b) A vessel restricted in her ability to manoeuvre, except a vessel engaged in mine clearance operations, shall exhibit:

(i) three all-round lights in a vertical line where they can best be seen. The highest and lowest of these lights shall be red and the middle light shall be white;

(ii) three shapes in a vertical line where they can best be seen. The highest and lowest of these shapes shall be balls and the middle one a diamond;

(iii) when making way through the water, a masthead light or lights, sidelights and a sternlight, in addition to the lights prescribed in sub-paragraph (i).

(iv) when at anchor, in addition to the lights or shapes prescribed in sub-paragraphs (i) and (ii), the light, lights or shape prescribed in Rule 30.

(c) A power-driven vessel engaged in a towing operation such as severely restricts the towing vessel and her tow in their ability to deviate from their course shall, in addition to the lights or shapes prescribed in Rule 24(a), exhibit the lights or shapes prescribed in sub-paragraphs (b)(i) and (ii) of this Rule.

(d) A vessel engaged in dredging or underwater operations, when restricted in her ability to manoeuvre, shall exhibit the lights and shapes prescribed in sub-paragraphs (b)(i), (ii) and (iii) of this Rule and shall in addition, when an obstruction exists, exhibit:

    (i) two all-round red lights or two balls in a vertical line to indicate the side on which the obstruction exists;

    (ii) two all-round green lights or two diamonds in a vertical line to indicate the side on which another vessel may pas;

    (iii) when at anchor, the lights or shapes prescribed in this paragraph instead of the lights or shape prescribed in Rule 30.

(e) Whenever the size of a vessel engaged in diving operations makes it impracticable to exhibit all lights and shapes prescribed in paragraph (d) of this Rule, the following shall be exhibited:

    (i) three all-round lights in a vertical line where they can best be seen. The highest and lowest of these lights shall be red and the middle light shall be white;

    (ii) a rigid replica of the International Code flag A, not less than 1 metre in height. Measures shall be taken to ensure its all-round visibility.

(f) A vessel engaged in mine clearance operations shall in addition to the lights prescribed for a power-driven vessel in Rule 23 or to the lights or shape prescribed for a vessel at anchor in Rule 30 as appropriate, exhibit three all-round green lights or three balls. One of these lights or shapes shall be exhibited near the foremast head and one at each end of the fore-yard. These lights or shapes indicate that it is dangerous for another vessel to approach within 1000 metres of the mine clearance vessel.

(g) Vessels of less than 12 metres in length, except those engaged in diving operations, shall not be required to exhibit the lights and shapes prescribed in this Rule.

(h) The signals prescribed in this Rule are not signals of vessels in distress and requiring assistance. Such signals are contained in Annex IV to these Regulations.

Rule 28
Vessels constrained by their draught

A vessel constrained by her draught may, in addition to the lights prescribed for power- driven vessels in Rule 23, exhibit where they can best be seen three all-round red lights in a vertical line, or a cylinder.

Rule 29
Pilot vessels

(a) A vessel engaged on pilotage duty shall exhibit:

    (i) at or near the masthead, two all-round lights in a vertical line, the upper being white and the lower red;

    (ii) when underway, in addition, sidelights and a sternlight;

    (iii) when at anchor, in addition to the lights prescribed in sub-paragraph (i), the light, lights or shape prescribed in Rule 30 for vessels at anchor.

(b) A pilot vessel when not engaged on pilotage duty shall exhibit the lights or shapes prescribed for a similar vessel of her length.

Rule 30
Anchored vessels and vessels aground

(a) A vessel at anchor shall exhibit where it can best be seen:

    (i) in the fore part, an all-round white light or one ball;

    (ii) at or near the stern and at a lower level than the light prescribed in sub-paragraph (i), an all-round white light.

(b) A vessel of less than 50 metres in length may exhibit an all-round white light where it can best be seen instead of the lights prescribed in paragraph (a) of this Rule.

(c) A vessel at anchor may, and a vessel of 100 metres and more in length shall, also use the available working or equivalent lights to illuminate her decks.

(d) A vessel aground shall exhibit the lights prescribed in paragraph (a) or (b) of this Rule and in addition, where they can best be seen:

(i) two all-round red lights in a vertical line;

(ii) three balls in a vertical line.

(e) A vessel of less than 7 metres in length, when at anchor not in or near a narrow channel, fairway or anchorage, or where other vessels normally navigate, shall not be required to exhibit the lights or shape prescribed in paragraphs (a) and (b) of this Rule.

(f) a vessel of less than 12 metres in length, when aground, shall not be required to exhibit the lights or shapes prescribed in sub-paragraphs (d)(i) and (ii) of this Rule.

Note to Rule 30

In the past, few yachtsmen have taken much notice of anchor balls, although, perhaps in the interests of self preservation, the Rule concerning anchor lights is generally observed. However, especially in waters used by commercial vessels, the observance of the Rule concerning anchor balls will help to minimise any antagonism between harbour masters, pilots and other professionals and the sport of sailing. It may be perfectly obvious to another yachtsman that a yacht is at anchor but from the bridge of a ship decisions have to be made at much greater distances and the pilot wants to know, at a glance, if the yacht is at anchor or motoring quietly up the river.

Rule 31
Seaplanes

Where it is impracticable for a seaplane to exhibit lights and shapes of the characteristics or in the positions prescribed in the Rules of this Part she shall exhibit lights and shapes as closely similar in characteristics and position as is possible.

Note to Rule 20-31

There are a great many different combinations of lights to denote different types and classes of vessels and some involved Rules about the siting, construction, arcs of visibility and visibility distances of lights. The yachtsman should know, in detail, what lights and day signals his own boat is required to carry and should also be able to recognise any other class or type of vessel by her lights or day signals. These lights and day signals are illustrated in the colour section of this book.

There are precise specifications in Annex I for the horizontal and vertical arcs through which lights must be visible. The regulations for vertical sectors of visibility are particularly important for sailing yachts, whose lights will be obscured at an appreciable angle of heel if they do not conform to these regulations. Sidelights are designed to show the aspect which a vessel is presenting. It is, therefore, important that the horizontal sectors should be correct if the sidelights are to do their job properly. In a small yacht, which uses sidelights mounted as a combined lantern, this means that a vertical filament bulb must be fitted.

Figs 11(a) & (b) overleaf illustrate the confusion that is likely to be caused by not having correct cut-offs to the horizontal arcs of visibility of the sidelights. Vessel A has sidelights which are each visible from 10° on the wrong bow. In *Fig 11(a)* an observer at B can see both the sidelights, and has the impression that A is steering directly towards him. In *Fig 11(b)*, A has altered course 15° to starboard but, because of the overlapping arcs of the sidelights, the observer at B can *still* see both of them and is unaware that A has made any alteration of course. This is a most unsatisfactory situation and one which can occur only as a result of fitting the wrong type of bulb in a combined lantern or having individual sidelights mounted so that their axis is not parallel to the fore and aft line of the boat.

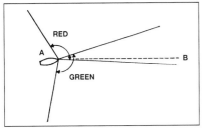

Fig 11(a)

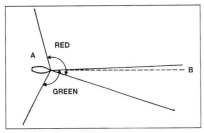

Fig 11(b)

Rule 25(b) which allows a sailing vessel under 20 metres in length to combine the sidelights and sternlight in one lantern fitted at or near the top of the mast is an extremely useful one. It means that a small yacht under sail can show all the lights required as one lantern, therefore using only half the electrical power that would be required for combined sidelights and a separate sternlight. This gives the yachtsman in a small sailing boat the opportunity to show a bright light without exhausting the battery during the course of a night at sea.

An auxiliary yacht which uses this tricolour lantern must, however, have an additional set of sidelights and a sternlight fitted lower down for use with a masthead (steaming) light when she is under power,

and needs to exhibit the lights for a power driven vessel. Thus it is sensible for an auxiliary sailing yacht to be equipped with a tri-colour light at the top of the mast as well as a combined port and starboard on the pulpit, a stern light and a masthead (steaming) light (at least one metre higher than the combined port and starboard lights). The separate stern light, and combined port and starboard lights, can then be used as emergency sailing lights in the event of a bulb or wiring failure in the tri-colour light.

The optional *masthead* red over green lights prescribed for a sailing vessel in Rule 25(c) are unlikely to be encountered very often, as they are extremely difficult to fit without making it impossible to hoist a burgee or fit a wind instrument at the masthead.

Note

The use of lights and shapes is illustrated in colour on pages 41 to 49.

PART D SOUND AND LIGHT SIGNALS

Rule 32
Definitions

(a) The word *whistle* means any sound signalling appliance capable of producing the prescribed blasts and which complies with the specifications in Annex III to these Regulations.

(b) The term *short blast* means a blast of about one second's duration.

(c) The term *prolonged blast* means a blast of from four to six seconds duration.

Rule 33
Equipment for sound signals

(a) A vessel of 12 metres or more in length shall be provided with a whistle and a bell and a vessel of 100 metres or more in length shall, in addition, be provided with a gong, the tone and sound of which cannot be confused with that of the bell. The whistle, bell and gong shall comply with the specifications in Annex III to these Regulations. The bell or gong or both may be replaced by other equipment having the same respective sound characteristics, provided that manual sounding of the prescribed signals shall always be possible.

(b) A vessel of less than 12 metres in length shall not be obliged to carry the sound signalling appliances prescribed in paragraph (a) of this Rule but if she does not, she shall be provided with some other means of making an efficient sound signal.

Note to Rule 33

Rule 33(b) allows the smaller vessel certain latitude in the type of sound signals which she may carry. The small aerosol type of fog signal has a number of points in its favour; it is easy to stow, simple to use, and relatively cheap. The majority are however, not really powerful enough to comply with the Rules nor are they very effective as a sound signal in fog.

The sophisticated hand or electrically operated sound signals are more difficult to install in a small yacht. They are, however, obviously more effective.

The choice between the various products on the market lies with each individual owner but he must realise that, if he takes a cheap and easy option, he cannot really expect his sound signal to be heard on board an approaching ship, against the background noise of machinery.

Rule 34
Manoeuvring and warning signals

(a) When vessels are in sight of one another, a power-driven vessel underway, when manoeuvring as authorized or required by these Rules, shall indicate that manoeuvre by the following signals on her whistle:

- one short blast to mean *I am altering my course to starboard;*

- two short blasts to mean *I am altering my course to port;*

- three short blasts to mean *I am operating astern propulsion.*

(b) Any vessel may supplement the whistle signals prescribed in paragraph (a) of this Rule by light signals, repeated as appropriate, whilst the manoeuvre is being carried out:

(i) these light signals shall have the following significance:

- one flash to mean *I am altering my course to starboard;*

- two flashes to mean *I am altering my course to port;*

- three flashes to mean *I am operating astern propulsion.*

(ii) the duration of each flash shall be about one second, the interval between flashes shall be about one second, and the interval between successive signals shall be not less than ten seconds.

(iii) the light used for this signal shall if fitted, be an all-round white light, visible at a minimum range of 5 miles, and shall comply with the provisions of Annex I to these Regulations.

(c) When in sight of one another in a narrow channel or fairway:

(i) a vessel intending to overtake another shall in compliance with Rule 9(e)(i) indicate her intention by the following signals on her whistle:

- two prolonged blasts followed by one short blast to mean *I intend to overtake you on your starboard side;*

- two prolonged blasts followed by two short blasts to mean *I intend to overtake you on your port side.*

(ii) the vessel about to be overtaken when acting in accordance with Rule 9(e)(i) shall indicate her agreement by the following signal on her whistle:

- one prolonged, one short, one prolonged and one short blast in that order.

(d) When vessels in sight of one another are approaching each other and from any cause either vessel fails to understand the intentions or actions of the other, or is in doubt whether sufficient action is being taken by the other to avoid collision, the vessel in doubt shall immediately indicate such doubt by giving at least five short and rapid blasts on the whistle. Such signal may be supplemented by a light signal of at least five short and rapid flashes.

(e) A vessel nearing a bend or an area of a channel or fairway where other vessels may be obscured by an intervening obstruction shall sound one prolonged blast. Such signal shall be answered with a prolonged blast by any approaching vessel that may be within hearing around the bend or behind the intervening obstruction.

(f) If whistles are fitted on a vessel at a distance apart of more than 100 metres, one whistle only shall be used for giving manoeuvring and warning signals.

Note to Rule 34

The only signal in this Rule that is likely to give rise to any confusion is the three short blasts, meaning *I am operating astern propulsion*. This means precisely what it says. A ship moving ahead at ten knots is perfectly correct to make the signal as soon as her engines are operating astern but she may continue to make headway for several minutes, and if she then stops her engines she may not gather sternway at all. The significance of this signal is, therefore, just as likely to be *I am slowing down as quickly as I can* as it is to be *I am about to gather sternway*.

Rule 35
Sound signals in restricted visibility

In or near an area of restricted visibility, whether by day or night, the signals prescribed in this Rule shall be used as follows:

(a) A power-driven vessel making way through the water shall sound at intervals of not more than 2 minutes one prolonged blast.

(b) A power-driven vessel underway but stopped and making no way through the water shall sound at intervals of not more than 2 minutes two prolonged blasts in succession with an interval of about 2 seconds between them.

(c) A vessel not under command, a vessel restricted in her ability to manoeuvre, a vessel constrained by her draught, a sailing vessel, a vessel engaged in fishing and a vessel engaged in towing or pushing another vessel shall, instead of the signals prescribed in paragraphs (a) or (b) of this Rule, sound at intervals of not more than 2 minutes three blasts in succession, namely one prolonged followed by two short blasts.

(d) A vessel engaged in fishing, when at anchor, and a vessel restricted in her ability to manoeuvre when carrying out her work at anchor, shall instead of the signals prescribed in paragraph (g) of this Rule, sound the signal prescribed in paragraph (c) of this Rule.

(e) A vessel towed or if more than one vessel is towed the last vessel of the tow, if manned, shall at intervals of not more than 2 minutes, sound four blasts in succession, namely one prolonged followed by three short blasts. When practicable, this signal shall be made immediately after the signal made by the towing vessel.

(f) When a pushing vessel and a vessel being pushed ahead are rigidly connected in a composite unit they shall be regarded as a power-driven vessel and shall give the signals prescribed in paragraphs (a) or (b) of this Rule.

(g) A vessel at anchor shall at intervals of not more than one minute ring the bell rapidly for about 5 seconds. In a vessel of 100 metres or more in length the bell shall be sounded in the forepart of the vessel and immediately after the ringing of the bell the gong shall be sounded rapidly for about 5 seconds in the after part of the vessel. A vessel at anchor may in addition sound three blasts in succession, namely one short, one prolonged and one short blast, to give warning of her position and of the possibility of collision to an approaching vessel.

(h) A vessel aground shall give the bell signal and if required the gong signal prescribed in paragraph (g) of this Rule and shall, in addition, give three separate and distinct strokes on the bell immediately before and after the rapid ringing of the bell. A vessel aground may in addition sound an appropriate whistle signal.

(i) A vessel of less than 12 metres in length shall not be obliged to give the above-mentioned signals but, if she does not, shall make some other efficient sound signal at intervals of not more than 2 minutes.

(j) A pilot vessel when engaged on pilotage duty may in addition to the signals prescribed in paragraphs (a), (b) or (g) of this Rule sound an identity signal consisting of four short blasts.

Note to Rule 35

Yachtsmen should particularly note that the sound signals for a sailing vessel in restricted visibility now take no account of which tack she happens to be on. Whatever her point of sailing there is only one signal.

Rule 36
Signals to attract attention

If necessary to attract the attention of another vessel any vessel may make light or sound signals that cannot be mistaken for any signal authorized elsewhere in these Rules, or may direct the beam of her searchlight in the direction of the danger, in such a way as not to embarrass any vessel.

Any light to attract the attention of another vessel shall be such that it cannot be mistaken for any aid to navigation. For the purpose of this Rule the use of high intensity intermittent or revolving lights, such as strobe lights, shall be avoided.

Note to Rule 36

The most usual occasion when a yacht skipper may wish to make use of this Rule is at night, in a shipping channel. Apart from the use of white flares, it is permissible to shine a light on the sails and to use a strong beamed light in the direction of the danger. For obvious reasons of night vision the words 'in such a way as not to embarrass any vessel' have been inserted in this Rule. To shine a beam directly at the bridge or wheelhouse of another vessel, at short range, may cause loss of night vision with disastrous consequences.

The reason for prohibiting a strobe light as a signal to attract attention is that such lights have a characteristic very similar to that of a north cardinal navigational mark.

Rule 37
Distress signals

When a vessel is in distress and requires assistance she shall use or exhibit the signals described in Annex IV to these regulations.

PART E EXEMPTIONS

Rule 38
Exemptions

Any vessel (or class of vessels) provided that she complies with the requirements of the International Regulations for Preventing Collisions at Sea, 1960, the keel of which is laid or which is at a corresponding stage of construction before the entry into force of these regulations may be exempted from compliance therewith as follows:

(a) The installation of lights with ranges prescribed in Rule 22, until four years after the date of entry into force of these Regulations.

(b) The installation of lights with colour specifications as prescribed in Section 7 of Annex I to these Regulations, until four years after the date of entry into force of these Regulations.

(c) The repositioning of lights as a result of conversion from Imperial to metric units and rounding off measurement figures, permanent exemption.

(d) (i) The repositioning of masthead lights on vessels of less than 150 metres in length, resulting from the prescriptions of Section 3(a) of Annex I to these Regulations permanent exemption;

    (ii) The re-positioning of masthead lights on vessels of 150 metres or more in length, resulting from the prescriptions of Section 3(a) of Annex I to these Regulations, until nine years after the date of entry into force of these Regulations.

(e) The repositioning of masthead lights resulting from the prescriptions of Section 2(b) of Annex I to these Regulations until nine years after the date of entry into force of these Regulations.

(f) The repositioning of sidelights resulting from the prescriptions of Sections 2(9) and 3(b) of Annex I to these Regulations until nine years after the date of entry into force of these Regulations.

(g) The requirements for sound signal appliances prescribed in Annex III to these Regulations, until nine years after the date of entry into force of these Regulations.

(h) The repositioning of all-round lights resulting from the prescription of Section 9 (b) of Annex I to these Regulations, permanent exemption.

Note to Rule 38

The exemptions listed are of very little significance to yachtsmen. They relate to changes in the Regulations concerning technical aspects of lights and sound signals.

ANNEX I

Positioning and technical details of lights and shapes

1. Definition

The term *height above the hull* means height above the uppermost continuous deck. This height shall be measured from the position vertically beneath the location of the light.

2. Vertical positioning and spacing of lights

(a) On a power-driven vessel of 20 metres or more in length the masthead lights shall be placed as follows:

(i) the forward masthead light, or if only one masthead light is carried, then that light, at a height above the hull of not less than 6 metres, and if the breadth of the vessel exceeds 6 metres, then at a height above the hull not less than such breadth, so however that the light need not be placed at a greater height above the hull than 12 metres;

(ii) when two masthead lights are carried the after one shall be at least 4.5 metres vertically higher than the forward one.

(b) The vertical separation of masthead lights of power-driven vessels shall be such that in all normal conditions of trim the after-light will be seen over and separate from the forward light at a distance of 1,000 metres from the stem when viewed from sea level.

(c) The masthead light of a power-driven vessel of 12 metres but less than 20 metres in length shall be placed at a height above the gunwale of not less than 2.5 metres.

(d) A power-driven vessel of less than 12 metres in length may carry the uppermost light at a height of less than 2.5 metres above the gunwale. When however a masthead light is carried in addition to sidelights and a sternlight or the all-round light of Rule 23(c)(i) is carried in addition to sidelights, then such masthead light or all-round light shall be carried at least 1 metre higher than the sidelights.

(e) One of the two or three masthead lights prescribed for a power-driven vessel when engaged in towing or pushing another vessel shall be placed in the same position as either the forward masthead light or the after masthead light; provided that, if carried on the aftermast, the lowest after masthead light shall be at least 4.5 metres vertically higher than the forward masthead light.

(f) (i) The masthead light or lights prescribed in Rule 23(a) shall be so placed as to be above and clear of all other lights and obstructions except as described in sub-paragraph (ii);

(ii) When it is impracticable to carry the all-round lights prescribed by Rule 27(b)(i) or Rule 28 below the masthead lights, they may be carried above the after masthead light(s) or vertically in between the forward masthead light(s) and after masthead light(s), provided that in the latter case the requirement of Section 3(c) of this Annex shall be complied with.

(g) The sidelights of a power-driven vessel shall be placed at a height above the hull not greater than three-quarters of that of the forward masthead light. They shall not be so low as to be interfered with by deck lights.

(h) The sidelights, if in a combined lantern and carried on a power-driven vessel of less than 20 metres in length shall be placed not less than 1 metre below the masthead light.

(i) When the Rules prescribe two or three lights to be carried in a vertical line they shall be space as follows:

  (i) on a vessel of 20 metres in length or more such lights shall be spaced not less than 2 metres apart, and the lowest of these lights shall, except where a towing light is required, be placed at a height of not less than four metres above the hull;

  (ii) on a vessel of less than 20 metres in length such lights shall be spaced not less than 1 metre apart and the lowest of these lights shall, except where a towing light is required, be placed at a height of not less than two metres above the gunwale;

  (iii) when three lights are carried they shall be equally spaced.

(j) The lower of the two all-round lights prescribed for a vessel when engaged in fishing shall be at a height above the sidelights not less than twice the distance between the two vertical lights.

(k) The forward anchor light prescribed in Rule 30(a)(i), when two are carried, shall not be less than 4.5 metres above the after one. On a vessel of 50 metres or more in length this forward anchor light shall be placed at a height of not less than 6 metres above the hull.

3. Horizontal positioning and spacing of lights

(a) When two masthead lights are prescribed for a power-driven vessel, the horizontal distance between them shall not be less than one-half of the length of the vessel but need not be more than 100 metres. The forward light shall be placed not more than one-quarter of the length of the vessel from the stem.

(b) On a power-driven vessel of 20 metres or more in length the sidelights shall not be placed in front of the forward masthead lights. They shall be placed at or near the side of the vessel.

(c) When the lights prescribed in Rule 27(b)(i) or Rule 28 are placed vertically between the forward masthead light(s) and the after masthead light(s) these all-round lights shall be placed at a horizontal distance of not less than 2 metres from the fore and aft centreline of the vessel in the athwartship direction.

(d) When only one masthead light is prescribed for a power driven vessel, this light shall be exhibited forward of amidships; except that a vessel of less than 20 metres in length need not exhibit this light forward of amidships but shall exhibit it as far forward as is practicable.

4. Details of location of direction-indicating lights for fishing vessels, dredgers and vessels engaged in underwater operations.

(a) The light indicating the direction of the outlying gear from a vessel engaged in fishing as prescribed in Rule 26(c)(ii) shall be placed at a horizontal distance of not less than 2 metres and not more than 6 metres away from the two all-round red and white lights. This light shall be placed not higher than the all-round white light prescribed in Rule 26(c)(i) and not lower than the sidelights.

(b) The lights and shapes on a vessel engaged in dredging or underwater operations to indicate the obstructed side and/or the side on which it is safe to pass, as prescribed in Rule 27(d)(i) and (ii), shall be placed at the maximum practical horizontal distance, but in no case less than 2 metres, from the lights or shapes prescribed in Rule 27(b)(i) and (ii). In no case shall the upper of these lights or shapes be at a greater height than the lower of the three lights or shapes prescribed in Rule 27(b)(i) and (ii).

5. Screens for sidelights

The sidelights of vessels of 20 metres or more in length shall be fitted with inboard screens painted matt black, and meeting the requirements of Section 9 of this Annex. On vessels of less than 20 metres in length the sidelights, if necessary to meet the requirements of Section 9 of this Annex, shall be fitted with inboard matt black screens. With a combined lantern, using a single vertical filament and a very narrow division between the green and red sections, external screens need not be fitted.

6. Shapes

(a) Shapes shall be black and of the following sizes:

  (i) a ball shall have a diameter of not less than 0.6 metre.

  (ii) a cone shall have a base diameter of not less than 0.6 metre and a height equal to its diameter.

  (iii) a cylinder shall have a diameter of at least 0.6 metre and a height of twice its diameter.

  (iv) a diamond shape shall consist of two cones as defined in (ii) above having a common base.

(b) The vertical distance between shapes shall be at least 1.5 metres.

(c) In a vessel of less than 20 metres in length shapes of lesser dimensions but commensurate with the size of the vessel may be used and the distance apart may be correspondingly reduced.

7. Colour specification of lights

The chromaticity of all navigation lights shall conform to the following standards, which lie within the boundaries of the area of the diagram specified for each colour by the International Commission on Illumination (CIE).

The boundaries of the area for each colour are given by indicating the corner co-ordinates, which are as follows below.

8. Intensity of lights

(a) The minimum luminous intensity of lights shall be calculated by using the formula:

$$I = 3.43 \times 10^6 \times T = D^2 \times K^{-D}$$

Where -

I is luminous intensity in candelas under service conditions,

T is threshold factor 2×10^{-7} lux,

D Is range of visibility (luminous range) of the light in nautical miles,

K is atmospheric transmissivity.

For prescribed lights the value of K shall be 0.8, corresponding to a meteorological visibility of approximately 13 nautical miles.

(b) A selection of figures derived from the formula is given in the following table:

Range of visibility (luminous range) of light in nautical miles D	Luminous intensity of light in candelas for K = 0.8 I
1	0.9
2	4.3
3	12.0
4	27.0
5	52.0
6	94.0

Note: The maximum luminous intensity of navigation lights should be limited to avoid undue glare. This shall not be achieved by a variable control of the luminous intensity.

(i) White	x 0.525	0.525	0.452	0.310	0.310	0.443
	y 0.382	0.440	0.440	0.348	0.283	0.382
(ii) Green	x 0.028 ·	0.009	0.300	0.203		
	y 0.385	0.723	0.511	0.356		
(iii) Red	x 0.680	0.660	0.735	0.721		
	y 0.320	0.320	0.265	0.259		
(iv) Yellow	x 0.612	0.618	0.575	0.575		
	y 0.382	0.382	0.425	0.406		

9. Horizontal sectors

(a) (i) In the forward direction, sidelights as fitted on the vessel shall show the minimum required intensities. The intensities must decrease to reach practical cut-off between 1 degree and 3 degrees outside the prescribed sectors.

(ii) For sternlights and masthead lights and at 22.5 degrees abaft the beam for sidelights, the minimum required intensities shall be maintained over the arc of the horizon up to 5 degrees within the limits of the sectors prescribed in Rule 21. From 5 degrees within the prescribed sectors the intensity may decrease by 50 per cent up to the prescribed limits; it shall decrease steadily to reach practical cut-off at not more than 5 degrees outside the prescribed sectors.

(b) (i) All-round lights shall be so located as not to be obscured by masts, topmasts or structures within angular sectors of more than 6 degrees, except anchor lights prescribed in Rule 30, which need not be placed at an impracticable height above the hull.

(ii) If it is impracticable to comply with paragraph (b)(i) of this section by exhibiting only one all-round light, two all-round lights shall be used suitably positioned or screened so that they appear, as far as practicable, as one light at a distance of one mile.

10. Vertical sectors

(a) The vertical sectors of electric lights as fitted, with the exception of lights on sailing vessels underway shall ensure that:

(i) at least the required minimum intensity is maintained at all angles from 5 degrees above to 5 degrees below the horizontal;

(ii) at least 60 per cent of the required minimum intensity is maintained from 7.5 degrees above to 7.5 degrees below the horizontal;

(b) In the case of sailing vessels underway the vertical sectors of electric lights as fitted shall ensure that:

(i) at least the required minimum intensity is maintained at all angles from 5 degrees above to 5 degrees below the horizontal;

(ii) at least 50 per cent of the required minimum intensity is maintained from 25 degrees above to 25 degrees below the horizontal.

(c) In the case of lights other than electric these specifications shall be met as closely as possible.

11. Intensity of non-electric lights

Non-electric lights shall so far as practicable comply with the minimum intensities, as specified in the Table given in Section 8 of this Annex.

12. Manoeuvring light

Notwithstanding the provisions of section 2(f) of this Annex the manoeuvring light described in Rule 34(b) shall be placed in the same fore and aft vertical plane as the masthead light or lights and, where practicable, at a minimum height of 2 metres vertically above the forward masthead light, provided that it shall be carried not less than 2 metres vertically above or below the after masthead light. On a vessel where only one masthead light is carried the manoeuvring light, if fitted, shall be carried where it can best be seen, not less than 2 metres vertically apart from the masthead light.

13. High speed craft

The masthead light of high speed craft with a length to breadth ratio of less than 3.0 may be placed at a height related to the breadth of the craft lower than that prescribed in paragraph 2(a)(i) of this annex, provided that the base angle of the isosceles triangles formed by the sidelights and masthead light, when seen in end elevation, is not less than 27°

14. Approval

The construction of lights and shapes and the installation of lights on board the vessel shall be to the satisfaction of the appropriate authority of the State whose flag the vessel is entitled to fly.

ANNEX II
Additional signals for fishing vessels fishing in close proximity

1. General

The lights mentioned herein shall, if exhibited in pursuance of Rule 26 (d), be placed where they can best be seen. They shall be at least 0.9 metre apart but at a lower level than lights prescribed in Rule 26(b)(i) and (c)(i). The lights shall be visible all round the horizon at a distance of at least 1 mile but a lesser distance than the lights prescribed by these Rules for fishing vessels.

2. Signals for trawlers

(a) Vessels of 20 metres or more in length when engaged in trawling, whether using demersal or pelagic gear, shall exhibit:

   (i) when shooting their nets:
        two white lights in a vertical line;

   (ii) when hauling their nets:
        one white light over one red light in a vertical line;

   (iii) when the net has come fast upon an obstruction:
        two red lights in a vertical line.

(b) Each vessel of 20 metres or more in length engaged in pair trawling shall exhibit:

   (i) by night, a searchlight directed forward and in the direction of the other vessel of the pair;

   (ii) when shooting or hauling their nets or when their nets have come fast upon an obstruction, the lights prescribed in 2(a) above.

(c) A vessel of less than 20 metres in length engaged in trawling, whether using demersal or pelagic gear or engaged in pair trawling, may exhibit the lights prescribed in paragraphs 2(a) or (b) of this section, as appropriate.

3. Signals for purse seiners

Vessels engaged in fishing with purse seine gear may exhibit two yellow lights in a vertical line. These lights shall flash alternately every second and with equal light and occultation duration. These lights may be exhibited only when the vessel is hampered by its fishing gear.

ANNEX III
Technical details of sound signal appliances

1. Whistles

(a) *Frequencies and range of audibility*

The fundamental frequency of the signal shall lie within the range 70-700 Hz.

The range of audibility of the signal from a whistle shall be determined by those frequencies, which may include the fundamental and/or one or more higher frequencies, which lie within the range 180-700 Hz (±1 per cent) and which provide the sound pressure levels specified in paragraph 1(c) below.

(b) *Limits of fundamental frequencies*

To ensure a wide variety of whistle characteristics, the fundamental frequency of a whistle shall be between the following limits:

   (i)   70-200 Hz, for a vessel 200 metres or more in length;

   (ii) 130-350 Hz, for a vessel 75 metres but less than 200 metres in length;

   (iii) 250-700 Hz, for a vessel less than 75 metres in length.

(c) *Sound signal intensity and range of audibility*

A whistle fitted in a vessel shall provide, in the direction of maximum intensity of the whistle and at a distance of 1 metre from it, a sound pressure level in at least one $1/3$rd-octave band within the range of frequencies 180-700 Hz (±1 per cent) of not less than the appropriate figure given in the table opposite.

The range of audibility in the table below is for information and is approximately the range at which a whistle may be heard on its forward axis with 90 per cent probability in conditions of still air on board a vessel having average background noise level at the listening posts (taken to be 68 dB in the octave band centred on 250 Hz and 63 dB in the octave band centred on 500 Hz).

In practice the range at which a whistle may be heard is extremely variable and depends critically on weather conditions; the values given can be regarded as typical but under conditions of strong wind or high ambient noise level at the listening post the range may be much reduced.

(d) *Directional properties*

The sound pressure level of a directional whistle shall be not more than 4 dB below the prescribed sound pressure level on the axis at any direction in the horizontal plane within ±45 degrees of the axis. The sound pressure level at any other direction in the horizontal plane shall be not more than 10 dB below the prescribed sound pressure level on the axis, so that the range in any direction will be at least half the range on the forward axis. The sound pressure level shall be measured in that $1/3$rd-octave band which determines the audibility

(e) *Positioning of whistles*

When a directional whistle is to be used as the only whistle on a vessel, it shall be installed with its maximum intensity directed straight ahead.

A whistle shall be placed as high as practicable on a vessel, in order to reduce interception of the emitted sound by obstructions and also to minimize hearing damage risk to personnel. The sound pressure level of the vessel's own signal at listening posts shall not exceed 110 dB (A) and so far as practicable should not 100 dB (A).

(f) *Fitting of more than one whistle*

If whistles are fitted at a distance apart of more than 100 metres, it shall be so arranged that they are not sounded simultaneously.

(g) *Combined whistle systems*

If due to the presence of obstructions the sound field of a single whistle, or of one of the whistles referred to in paragraph 1(f) above, is likely to have a zone of greatly reduced signal level, it is recommended that a combined whistle system be fitted so as to overcome this reduction. For the purposes of the Rules a combined whistle system is to be regarded as a single whistle. The whistles of a combined system shall be located at a distance apart of not more than 100 metres and arranged to be sounded simultaneously. The frequency of any one whistle shall differ from those of the others by at least 10 Hz.

2. Bell or gong

(a) *Intensity of signal*

A bell or gong, or other device having similar sound characteristics shall produce a sound pressure level of not less than 100 dB at a distance of 1 metre from it.

(b) *Construction*

Bells and gongs shall be made of corrosion-resistant material and designed to give a clear tone. The diameter of the mouth of the bell shall be not less than 300mm for vessels of 20 metres or more in length and shall be not less than   200mm for vessels of 12 metres or more but of less than 20 metres in length. Where practicable, a power-driven bell striker is recommended to ensure constant force but manual operation shall be possible. The mass of the striker shall be not less than 3 per cent of the mass of the bell.

3. Approval

The construction of sound signal appliances, their performance and their installation on board the vessel shall be to the satisfaction of the appropriate authority of the State whose flag the vessel is entitled to fly.

Length of vessel in metres	$1/3$rd-octave band level at 1 metre in dB referred to 2×10^{-5} N/m^2	Audibility range in nautical miles
200 or more	143	2.0
75 but less than 200	138	1.5
20 but less than 75	130	1.0
Less than 20	120	0.5

ANNEX IV
Distress signals

1. The following signals, used or exhibited either together or separately, indicate distress and need of assistance:

(a) a gun or other explosive signal fired at intervals of about a minute.

(b) a continuous sounding with any fog-signalling apparatus.

(c) rockets or shells, throwing red stars fired one at a time at short intervals.

(d) a signal made by radiotelegraphy or by any other signalling method consisting of the group • • • — — — • • • (SOS) in the Morse Code.

(e) a signal sent by radiotelephony consisting of the spoken word "Mayday".

(f) the International Code Signal of distress indicated by N.C.

(g) a signal consisting of a square flag having above or below it a ball or anything resembling a ball.

(h) flames on the vessel (as from a burning tar barrel, oil barrel, etc).

(i) a rocket parachute flare or a hand flare showing a red light.

(j) a smoke signal giving off orange-coloured smoke.

(k) slowly and repeatedly raising and lowering arms outstretched to each side.

(l) the radiotelegraph alarm signal.

(m) the radiotelephone alarm signal.

(n) signals transmitted by emergency position-indicating radio beacons.

(o) approved signals transmitted by radio communication systems, including survival craft radar transponders.

2. The use or exhibition of any of the foregoing signals except for the purpose of indicating distress and need of assistance and the use of other signals which may be confused with any of the above signals is prohibited.

3. Attention is drawn to relevant sections of the International Code of Signals, the Merchant Ship Search and Rescue Manual and the following signals:

(a) a piece of orange-coloured canvas with either a black square and circle or other appropriate symbol (for identification from the air).

(b) a dye marker.

LIGHTS AND SHAPES SUPPLEMENT

LIGHTS FOR MOTOR YACHTS

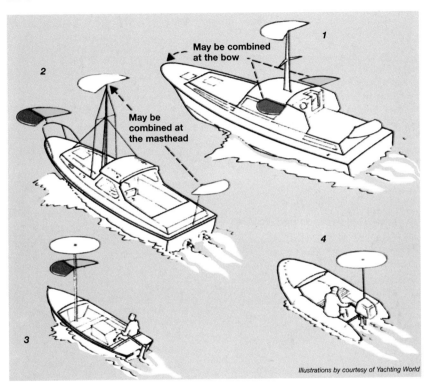

Illustrations by courtesy of Yachting World

The exact specification of the lights for a motor yacht depends upon the length of the boat. In general, the lights consist of a white masthead light, visible 112.5° either side of the bow, red and green sidelights, each visible from right ahead to 112.5° on the bow and a white sternlight visible 67.5° either side of right astern.

1 12-20 metres LOA.

Masthead light visible three miles, mounted at least 2.5 metres above the sidelights. Sidelights mounted as separate lanterns or as a combined lantern and both sidelights and sternlight visible two miles.

2 Under 12 metres LOA.

Masthead light and sternlight, visible two miles and masthead light mounted at least one metre above the sidelights. Sidelights visible one mile and may be combined in a single lantern. The masthead light and stern light may be combined in a single lantern, at or near the masthead.

3 & 4 Under 7 metres LOA, maximum speed not exceeding 7 knots.

Obliged to carry only an all-round white light, visible two miles, but should, if practicable, also carry sidelights.

LIGHTS FOR SAILING YACHTS

Vessels under sail are required to carry only sidelights and a sternlight. In yachts under 20 metres they may be combined in a single lantern at the masthead. A sailing vessel may also show an all-round red light over an all-round green light at the masthead but these optional lights are very seldom fitted. As the majority of sea-going yachts are auxiliaries, provision must be made to carry both the lights for a sailing vessel and a power-driven vessel. It is important in most sailing yachts that the navigation lights should place the least possible demand on the battery. The lights which are recommended in order to meet this requirement are:

Fig A
Vessels under 20 metres

Lantern 1A alone meets the requirements when under sail, with minimum battery drain.

Lanterns 3 and 4 provide an alternative if Lantern 1A fails.

Lanterns 2, 3 and 4 together are required when under power.

An anchor light, all round white, is also required.

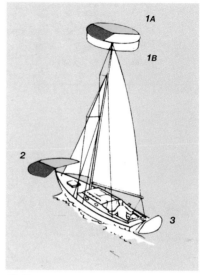

Fig B

Fig B
Vessels under 12 metres

Lantern 1 consists of a tricolour light (1A), mounted directly above, and switchable independently of an all-round white light (1B).

Lantern 1A, used by itself, meets the requirements when under sail.
Lanterns 1B and 2 are used together when under power.

Lantern 1B alone may be used as an anchor light.

Lantern 3 is not strictly necessary, but if it is fitted **Lanterns 2 and 3** together provide an alternative to 1A in the event of bulb-failure at the masthead, which may be difficult to rectify in a sea-way.

In yachts fitted with both a masthead-mounted tricolour lantern (1A) and a combind port-and-starboard lantern at deck level (2) it is important to ensure that the switch-panel is clearly labelled. Increasing instances are seen in which yachts sail with both upper and lower lights switched on. This is wrong and causes confusion.

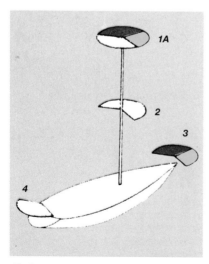

Fig A

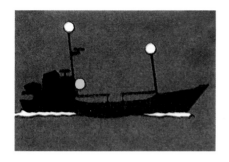

A power driven vessel, probably over 50 metres. On a dark night the aspect of the vessel can be **estImated** by the relative positions of the masthead lights.

A vessel under 50 metres is obliged to show only one masthead light and her aspect is consequently more difficult to estimate.

A small boat under oars need show only a lantern or electric torch *In sufficient time to prevent collision*.

A sailing vessel under auxiliary power is a power driven vessel and must show the appropriate lights.

Sailing yachts, with lights mounted low down, may be visible only intermittently in a seaway.

The greater height of a masthead combined lantern improves the visibility of a yacht's lights at sea.

A tug and tow seen from the starboard quarter. The yellow light above the white sternlight identifies the tug. By day, if the length of the tow is over 200 metres, both will show a diamond shape.

A tug and tow seen from directly ahead. The two masthead lights in a vertical line on the tug show that she is towing, although from this aspect it is not immediately obvious that the higher light is not the normal after masthead light of a ship over 50 metres in length.

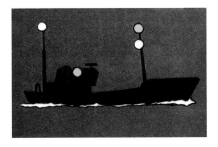

A vessel engaged in trawling. She should be given a wide berth, as she may manoeuvre unpredictably when hauling her net. By day, all vessels engaged in fishing show a shape consisting of two cones, apexes together.

A vessel engaged in fishing, other than trawling. If she had gear extending more than 150 metres horizontally into the seaway she would show another, lower, white light indicating the direction of her gear. This light would be replaced by a cone, apex up, by day.

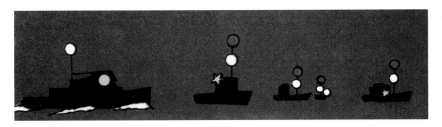

Fishing vessels frequently work as a fleet. It is often safer to go round the fleet than to try to find a way through.

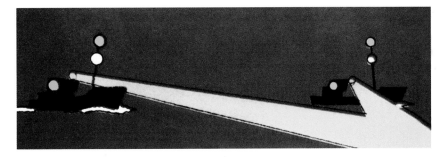

The special signal for two fishing vessels pair trawling.

A vessel restricted in her ability to manoeuvre. The masthead lights and side lights show that she is making way through the water. By day she would show a ball over a diamond over a ball, in place of the red over white over red lights.

A tug and tow, restricted in their ability to manoeuvre. The three masthead lights of the tug show that the length of the tow is more than 200 metres.

A dredger at work. The two red lights in a vertical line show that she is foul on that side. The two green lights show that that side is clear of obstructions. By day, the red lights would be replaced by balls and the green lights by diamonds.

A vessel constrained by her draught and thus severely restricted in ability to deviate from her course. By day the three red lights would be replaced by a cylinder.

A vessel not under command. By night she would show two, all-round, red lights in a vertical line in place of the two balls.

A minesweeper with gear streamed on both quarters. By night, each of the three balls would be replaced by a green light. It is dangerous to approach within 500 metres on either side, or 1000 metres astern.

A vessel aground. By night, she would show anchor lights and two, all-round, red lights in a vertical line.

A vessel engaged in pilotage duty, at anchor. The single white light is her anchor light, which would be replaced by a ball by day, and the white over red are her pilotage lights.

Great care must be taken in a busy harbour at night, as navigation and anchor lights tend to merge with the background of shore lights.

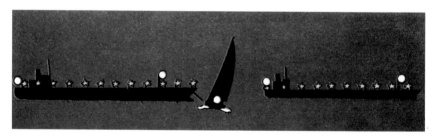

Vessels over 100 metres long, at anchor, are required to switch on their deck working lights. Other, less bright, lights in their vicinity are very difficult to see.

A small vessel engaged in diving operations. For the safety of her divers, she must be given a wide berth.

Illustrations by courtesy of Yachting World

RYA *Membership*

Promoting and Protecting Boating
www.rya.org.uk

The RYA is the national organisation which represents the interests of everyone who goes boating for pleasure.

The greater the membership, the louder our voice when it comes to protecting members' interests.

Apply for membership today, and support the RYA, to help the RYA support you.

and Protecting Boating

Benefits of Membership

- Access to expert advice on all aspects of boating from legal wrangles to training matters

- Special members' discounts on a range of products and services including boat insurance, books, videos and class certificates

- Free issue of certificates of competence, increasingly asked for by everyone from overseas governments to holiday companies, insurance underwriters to boat hirers

- Access to the wide range of RYA publications, including the quarterly magazine

- Third Party insurance for windsurfing members

- Free Internet access with RYA-Online

- A privilege price structure for purchasing a Volvo car

- Regular offers in RYA Magazine

- ...and much more

Join online at *www.rya.org.uk*
or use the form overleaf.

Visit the website for information, advice, member services and web shop.

If you have previously been a member and know your membership number please enter here

When completed, please send this form to: RYA RYA House Ensign Way Hamble Southampton SO31 4YA

	Tick box	Cash/Chq.	DD
Family		£44	£41
Personal		£28	£25
Under 21		£11	£11

Please indicate your main area of interest

- ❏ Yacht Racing
- ❏ Yacht Cruising
- ❏ Dinghy Racing
- ❏ Dinghy Cruising
- ❏ Personal Watercraft
- ❏ Inland Waterways
- ❏ Powerboat Racing
- ❏ Windsurfing
- ❏ Motor Boating
- ❏ Sportsboats and RIBs

† Family Membership = 2 adults plus any U21's all living at the same address.

For details of Life Membership and paying over the phone by Credit/Debit card, please call 0845 345 0374/5 or join online at www.rya.org.uk

PLEASE USE BLOCK CAPITALS

Title	Forename	Surname	Date of Birth	Male	Female
1.					
2.					
3.					
4.					

Address

Town   County   Postcode

Home Phone No.   Day Phone No.

Facsimile No.   Mobile No.

Email Address

Signature   Date

DISCOUNT IF YOU PAY BY DIRECT DEBIT - SEE ABOVE

RYA

Instructions to your Bank or Building Society to pay by Direct Debit

DIRECT Debit

Please fill in the form and send to:
RYA RYA House Ensign Way Hamble Southampton SO31 4YA Tel: 0845 345 0400

Name and full postal address of your Bank/Building Society

To The Manager   Bank/Building Society

Address

Postcode

Name(s) of Account Holder(s)

Bank/Building Society account number

Branch Sort Code

Originator's Identification Number

9	5	5	2	1	3

Reference Number

Instruction to your Bank or Building Society
Please pay Royal Yachting Association Direct Debits from the account detailed in this instruction subject to the safeguards assured by The Direct Debit Guarantee. I understand that this instruction may remain with the Royal Yachting Association and, if so, details will be passed electronically to my Bank/Building Society.

Signature(s)

Date

Banks and Building Societies may not accept Direct Debit Instructions for some types of account

---

OR YOU CAN PAY BY CHEQUE

Source Code
077

Cheque enclosed   £   Made payable to the 'RYA'

Office use only: Membership number allocated

expert
knowledge
and
advice
online

RYA Shop

RYA

www.rya.org.uk